ISBN: 978-1-954608-08-5

Our Humble Request:

We Love Feedback, please do consider leaving us a review! Also, we'd Love to stay in touch, please visit our website: https://www.tiesthatbindpublishing.com

If you're ever in the neighborhood, drop by and visit us on our social media!

Facebook: https://bit.ly/3slmA7N
Instagram: https://bit.ly/3dEXQ6i
Twitter: https://Twitter.com/ttbp20
YouTube: https://bit.ly/37CukdN

Forget Me Not: Password & Username Journal

By: LaTia & William Russell

This P & U Belongs To:

Intro:

Did you know, most people have up to 100 passwords to remember?! Talk about a brain workout...but let's be honest, having to manage passwords stinks! If you're anything like us, you have a gazillion usernames and passwords, all with different requirements! Some require 6-20 letters, numbers, special character sequences (uppercase, lowercase... backwards.... HA!). Others require more or less than above without special characters or only particular characters. How can you keep up?! No, seriously, how? If I had $1 for every time, I had to.... yep, you guessed it, reset my password. Well, I would probably be writing this introduction from the beach instead of the current, snowy, frigid climate that I'm currently in. Just this past week, I must've hit my personal best in having to reset my password for various areas of my life that I need to access electronically. That got me thinking, why isn't there something nice and neat already available to help me keep up with all of this information?! Then *Ding* the light bulb came on, create said thing, to help your fellow human (or other being depending on how you identify; we're all about inclusivity here) do just that. So, here you go, our gift to you...your P (password) & U (username) tracker (see what we did there, "P...U...)! You can thank us by purchasing a ton, so we can create the next thing you desperately need to make your life easier from the beach (we're kidding.... kind of)!

We've given you what you need, the rest is up to you! Happy Tracking!

Password & Username Tracker

Email (Personal & Professional)

Website:____

Username:____

Password:____

Last 3 Passwords:______________________________________

Important to Note (i.e. date reminder):_______________________

____

Website:____

Username:____

Password:____

Last 3 Passwords:______________________________________

Important to Note (i.e. date reminder):_______________________

____

Website:____

Username:____

Password:____

Last 3 Passwords:______________________________________

Important to Note (i.e. date reminder):_______________________

____

Email (Personal & Professional)

Website:____

Username:______________________________________

Password:_______________________________________

Last 3 Passwords:________________________________

Important to Note (i.e. date reminder):____________________

____

Website:____

Username:______________________________________

Password:_______________________________________

Last 3 Passwords:________________________________

Important to Note (i.e. date reminder):____________________

____

Website:____

Username:______________________________________

Password:_______________________________________

Last 3 Passwords:________________________________

Important to Note (i.e. date reminder):____________________

____

Email (Personal & Professional)

Website:____

Username:____

Password:____

Last 3 Passwords:______________________________________

Important to Note (i.e. date reminder):_________________________

____

Website:____

Username:____

Password:____

Last 3 Passwords:______________________________________

Important to Note (i.e. date reminder):_________________________

____

Website:____

Username:____

Password:____

Last 3 Passwords:______________________________________

Important to Note (i.e. date reminder):_________________________

____

Email (Personal & Professional)

Website:________________________________

Username:________________________________

Password:________________________________

Last 3 Passwords:____________________________

Important to Note (i.e. date reminder):____________________

____

Website:________________________________

Username:________________________________

Password:________________________________

Last 3 Passwords:____________________________

Important to Note (i.e. date reminder):____________________

____

Website:________________________________

Username:________________________________

Password:________________________________

Last 3 Passwords:____________________________

Important to Note (i.e. date reminder):____________________

____

Email (Personal & Professional)

Website:____

Username:____

Password:____

Last 3 Passwords:_______________________________________

Important to Note (i.e. date reminder):_________________________

____

Website:____

Username:____

Password:____

Last 3 Passwords:_______________________________________

Important to Note (i.e. date reminder):_________________________

____

Website:____

Username:____

Password:____

Last 3 Passwords:_______________________________________

Important to Note (i.e. date reminder):_________________________

____

Email (Personal & Professional)

Website:____

Username:______________________________________

Password:_______________________________________

Last 3 Passwords:_________________________________

Important to Note (i.e. date reminder):____________________

____

Website:____

Username:______________________________________

Password:_______________________________________

Last 3 Passwords:_________________________________

Important to Note (i.e. date reminder):____________________

____

Website:____

Username:______________________________________

Password:_______________________________________

Last 3 Passwords:_________________________________

Important to Note (i.e. date reminder):____________________

____

Email (Personal & Professional)

Website:____

Username:______________________________________

Password:_______________________________________

Last 3 Passwords:__________________________________

Important to Note (i.e. date reminder):____________________

____

Website:____

Username:______________________________________

Password:_______________________________________

Last 3 Passwords:__________________________________

Important to Note (i.e. date reminder):____________________

____

Website:____

Username:______________________________________

Password:_______________________________________

Last 3 Passwords:__________________________________

Important to Note (i.e. date reminder):____________________

____

Email (Personal & Professional)

Website:____

Username:____

Password:____

Last 3 Passwords:____

Important to Note (i.e. date reminder):____

____

Website:____

Username:____

Password:____

Last 3 Passwords:____

Important to Note (i.e. date reminder):____

____

Website:____

Username:____

Password:____

Last 3 Passwords:____

Important to Note (i.e. date reminder):____

____

Email (Personal & Professional)

Website:____

Username:____

Password:____

Last 3 Passwords:_____________________________________

Important to Note (i.e. date reminder):_______________________

____

Website:____

Username:____

Password:____

Last 3 Passwords:_____________________________________

Important to Note (i.e. date reminder):_______________________

____

Website:____

Username:____

Password:____

Last 3 Passwords:_____________________________________

Important to Note (i.e. date reminder):_______________________

____

Email (Personal & Professional)

Website:____

Username:____

Password:____

Last 3 Passwords:_______________________________________

Important to Note (i.e. date reminder):_______________________

____

Website:____

Username:____

Password:____

Last 3 Passwords:_______________________________________

Important to Note (i.e. date reminder):_______________________

____

Website:____

Username:____

Password:____

Last 3 Passwords:_______________________________________

Important to Note (i.e. date reminder):_______________________

____

Social Media (i.e., FB, IG, Twitter, etc.;)

Website:____

Username:______________________________________

Password:_______________________________________

Last 3 Passwords:_________________________________

Important to Note (i.e. date reminder):______________________

____

Website:____

Username:______________________________________

Password:_______________________________________

Last 3 Passwords:_________________________________

Important to Note (i.e. date reminder):______________________

____

Website:____

Username:______________________________________

Password:_______________________________________

Last 3 Passwords:_________________________________

Important to Note (i.e. date reminder):______________________

____

Social Media (i.e., FB, IG, Twitter, etc.;)

Website:____

Username:_______________________________________

Password:_______________________________________

Last 3 Passwords:__________________________________

Important to Note (i.e. date reminder):____________________

____

Website:____

Username:_______________________________________

Password:_______________________________________

Last 3 Passwords:__________________________________

Important to Note (i.e. date reminder):____________________

____

Website:____

Username:_______________________________________

Password:_______________________________________

Last 3 Passwords:__________________________________

Important to Note (i.e. date reminder):____________________

____

Social Media (i.e., FB, IG, Twitter, etc.;)

Website:____

Username:______________________________________

Password:______________________________________

Last 3 Passwords:________________________________

Important to Note (i.e. date reminder):____________________

____

Website:____

Username:______________________________________

Password:______________________________________

Last 3 Passwords:________________________________

Important to Note (i.e. date reminder):____________________

____

Website:____

Username:______________________________________

Password:______________________________________

Last 3 Passwords:________________________________

Important to Note (i.e. date reminder):____________________

____

Social Media (i.e., FB, IG, Twitter, etc.;)

Website:____

Username:____

Password:____

Last 3 Passwords:______________________________________

Important to Note (i.e. date reminder):_______________________

____

Website:____

Username:____

Password:____

Last 3 Passwords:______________________________________

Important to Note (i.e. date reminder):_______________________

____

Website:____

Username:____

Password:____

Last 3 Passwords:______________________________________

Important to Note (i.e. date reminder):_______________________

____

Social Media (i.e., FB, IG, Twitter, etc.;)

Website:____

Username:______________________________________

Password:_______________________________________

Last 3 Passwords:__________________________________

Important to Note (i.e. date reminder):____________________

Website:____

Username:______________________________________

Password:_______________________________________

Last 3 Passwords:__________________________________

Important to Note (i.e. date reminder):____________________

Website:____

Username:______________________________________

Password:_______________________________________

Last 3 Passwords:__________________________________

Important to Note (i.e. date reminder):____________________

Social Media (i.e., FB, IG, Twitter, etc.;)

Website:____

Username:_______________________________________

Password:_______________________________________

Last 3 Passwords:__________________________________

Important to Note (i.e. date reminder):____________________

____

Website:____

Username:_______________________________________

Password:_______________________________________

Last 3 Passwords:__________________________________

Important to Note (i.e. date reminder):____________________

____

Website:____

Username:_______________________________________

Password:_______________________________________

Last 3 Passwords:__________________________________

Important to Note (i.e. date reminder):____________________

____

Social Media (i.e., FB, IG, Twitter, etc.;)

Website:______________________________________

Username:_____________________________________

Password:_____________________________________

Last 3 Passwords:________________________________

Important to Note (i.e. date reminder):____________________

____

Website:______________________________________

Username:_____________________________________

Password:_____________________________________

Last 3 Passwords:________________________________

Important to Note (i.e. date reminder):____________________

____

Website:______________________________________

Username:_____________________________________

Password:_____________________________________

Last 3 Passwords:________________________________

Important to Note (i.e. date reminder):____________________

____

Social Media (i.e., FB, IG, Twitter, etc.;)

Website:______________________________

Username:______________________________

Password:______________________________

Last 3 Passwords:__________________________

Important to Note (i.e. date reminder):________________

____

Website:______________________________

Username:______________________________

Password:______________________________

Last 3 Passwords:__________________________

Important to Note (i.e. date reminder):________________

____

Website:______________________________

Username:______________________________

Password:______________________________

Last 3 Passwords:__________________________

Important to Note (i.e. date reminder):________________

____

Social Media (i.e., FB, IG, Twitter, etc.;)

Website:________________________________

Username:______________________________

Password:______________________________

Last 3 Passwords:__________________________

Important to Note (i.e. date reminder):________________

____

Website:________________________________

Username:______________________________

Password:______________________________

Last 3 Passwords:__________________________

Important to Note (i.e. date reminder):________________

____

Website:________________________________

Username:______________________________

Password:______________________________

Last 3 Passwords:__________________________

Important to Note (i.e. date reminder):________________

____

Social Media (i.e., FB, IG, Twitter, etc.;)

Website:____

Username:______________________________________

Password:_______________________________________

Last 3 Passwords:__________________________________

Important to Note (i.e. date reminder):____________________

____

Website:____

Username:______________________________________

Password:_______________________________________

Last 3 Passwords:__________________________________

Important to Note (i.e. date reminder):____________________

____

Website:____

Username:______________________________________

Password:_______________________________________

Last 3 Passwords:__________________________________

Important to Note (i.e. date reminder):____________________

____

Finance (i.e., Online Banking, credit cards, etc.;)

Website:____

Username:______________________________________

Password:______________________________________

Last 3 Passwords:__________________________________

Important to Note (i.e. date reminder):____________________

____

Website:____

Username:______________________________________

Password:______________________________________

Last 3 Passwords:__________________________________

Important to Note (i.e. date reminder):____________________

____

Website:____

Username:______________________________________

Password:______________________________________

Last 3 Passwords:__________________________________

Important to Note (i.e. date reminder):____________________

____

Finance (i.e., Online Banking, credit cards, etc.;)

Website:____

Username:______________________________________

Password:______________________________________

Last 3 Passwords:__________________________________

Important to Note (i.e. date reminder):____________________

Website:____

Username:______________________________________

Password:______________________________________

Last 3 Passwords:__________________________________

Important to Note (i.e. date reminder):____________________

Website:____

Username:______________________________________

Password:______________________________________

Last 3 Passwords:__________________________________

Important to Note (i.e. date reminder):____________________

Finance (i.e., Online Banking, credit cards, etc.;)

Website:____

Username:______________________________________

Password:______________________________________

Last 3 Passwords:_________________________________

Important to Note (i.e. date reminder):____________________

____

Website:____

Username:______________________________________

Password:______________________________________

Last 3 Passwords:_________________________________

Important to Note (i.e. date reminder):____________________

____

Website:____

Username:______________________________________

Password:______________________________________

Last 3 Passwords:_________________________________

Important to Note (i.e. date reminder):____________________

____

Finance (i.e., Online Banking, credit cards, etc.;)

Website:____

Username:____

Password:____

Last 3 Passwords:_______________________________________

Important to Note (i.e. date reminder):_________________________

____

Website:____

Username:____

Password:____

Last 3 Passwords:_______________________________________

Important to Note (i.e. date reminder):_________________________

____

Website:____

Username:____

Password:____

Last 3 Passwords:_______________________________________

Important to Note (i.e. date reminder):_________________________

____

Finance (i.e., Online Banking, credit cards, etc.;)

Website:____

Username:______________________________________

Password:______________________________________

Last 3 Passwords:__________________________________

Important to Note (i.e. date reminder):____________________

____

Website:____

Username:______________________________________

Password:______________________________________

Last 3 Passwords:__________________________________

Important to Note (i.e. date reminder):____________________

____

Website:____

Username:______________________________________

Password:______________________________________

Last 3 Passwords:__________________________________

Important to Note (i.e. date reminder):____________________

____

Finance (i.e., Online Banking, credit cards, etc.;)

Website:____

Username:_______________________________________

Password:_______________________________________

Last 3 Passwords:__________________________________

Important to Note (i.e. date reminder):____________________

____

Website:____

Username:_______________________________________

Password:_______________________________________

Last 3 Passwords:__________________________________

Important to Note (i.e. date reminder):____________________

____

Website:____

Username:_______________________________________

Password:_______________________________________

Last 3 Passwords:__________________________________

Important to Note (i.e. date reminder):____________________

____

Finance (i.e., Online Banking, credit cards, etc.;)

Website:____

Username:______________________________________

Password:______________________________________

Last 3 Passwords:_________________________________

Important to Note (i.e. date reminder):____________________

____

Website:____

Username:______________________________________

Password:______________________________________

Last 3 Passwords:_________________________________

Important to Note (i.e. date reminder):____________________

____

Website:____

Username:______________________________________

Password:______________________________________

Last 3 Passwords:_________________________________

Important to Note (i.e. date reminder):____________________

____

Finance (i.e., Online Banking, credit cards, etc.;)

Website:________________________________

Username:________________________________

Password:________________________________

Last 3 Passwords:____________________________

Important to Note (i.e. date reminder):__________________

____

Website:________________________________

Username:________________________________

Password:________________________________

Last 3 Passwords:____________________________

Important to Note (i.e. date reminder):__________________

____

Website:________________________________

Username:________________________________

Password:________________________________

Last 3 Passwords:____________________________

Important to Note (i.e. date reminder):__________________

____

Finance (i.e., Online Banking, credit cards, etc.;)

Website:____

Username:______________________________________

Password:______________________________________

Last 3 Passwords:_________________________________

Important to Note (i.e. date reminder):____________________

____

Website:____

Username:______________________________________

Password:______________________________________

Last 3 Passwords:_________________________________

Important to Note (i.e. date reminder):____________________

____

Website:____

Username:______________________________________

Password:______________________________________

Last 3 Passwords:_________________________________

Important to Note (i.e. date reminder):____________________

____

Finance (i.e., Online Banking, credit cards, etc.;)

Website:____

Username:______________________________________

Password:_______________________________________

Last 3 Passwords:__________________________________

Important to Note (i.e. date reminder):____________________

____

Website:____

Username:______________________________________

Password:_______________________________________

Last 3 Passwords:__________________________________

Important to Note (i.e. date reminder):____________________

____

Website:____

Username:______________________________________

Password:_______________________________________

Last 3 Passwords:__________________________________

Important to Note (i.e. date reminder):____________________

____

Utilities (i.e., wi-fi, electricity, etc.;)

Website:____

Username:______________________________________

Password:_______________________________________

Last 3 Passwords:__________________________________

Important to Note (i.e. date reminder):______________________

____

Website:____

Username:______________________________________

Password:_______________________________________

Last 3 Passwords:__________________________________

Important to Note (i.e. date reminder):______________________

____

Website:____

Username:______________________________________

Password:_______________________________________

Last 3 Passwords:__________________________________

Important to Note (i.e. date reminder):______________________

____

Utilities (i.e., wi-fi, electricity, etc.;)

Website:____

Username:____

Password:____

Last 3 Passwords:____

Important to Note (i.e. date reminder):____________________

____

Website:____

Username:____

Password:____

Last 3 Passwords:____

Important to Note (i.e. date reminder):____________________

____

Website:____

Username:____

Password:____

Last 3 Passwords:____

Important to Note (i.e. date reminder):____________________

____

Utilities (i.e., wi-fi, electricity, etc.;)

Website:____

Username:______________________________________

Password:______________________________________

Last 3 Passwords:_________________________________

Important to Note (i.e. date reminder):____________________

____

Website:____

Username:______________________________________

Password:______________________________________

Last 3 Passwords:_________________________________

Important to Note (i.e. date reminder):____________________

____

Website:____

Username:______________________________________

Password:______________________________________

Last 3 Passwords:_________________________________

Important to Note (i.e. date reminder):____________________

____

Utilities (i.e., wi-fi, electricity, etc.;)

Website:________________________________

Username:_______________________________

Password:_______________________________

Last 3 Passwords:___________________________

Important to Note (i.e. date reminder):_______________

____

Website:________________________________

Username:_______________________________

Password:_______________________________

Last 3 Passwords:___________________________

Important to Note (i.e. date reminder):_______________

____

Website:________________________________

Username:_______________________________

Password:_______________________________

Last 3 Passwords:___________________________

Important to Note (i.e. date reminder):_______________

____

Utilities (i.e., wi-fi, electricity, etc.;)

Website:____

Username:______________________________________

Password:______________________________________

Last 3 Passwords:__________________________________

Important to Note (i.e. date reminder):____________________

____

Website:____

Username:______________________________________

Password:______________________________________

Last 3 Passwords:__________________________________

Important to Note (i.e. date reminder):____________________

____

Website:____

Username:______________________________________

Password:______________________________________

Last 3 Passwords:__________________________________

Important to Note (i.e. date reminder):____________________

____

Utilities (i.e., wi-fi, electricity, etc.;)

Website:______________________________

Username:______________________________

Password:______________________________

Last 3 Passwords:______________________________

Important to Note (i.e. date reminder):______________________________

____

Website:______________________________

Username:______________________________

Password:______________________________

Last 3 Passwords:______________________________

Important to Note (i.e. date reminder):______________________________

____

Website:______________________________

Username:______________________________

Password:______________________________

Last 3 Passwords:______________________________

Important to Note (i.e. date reminder):______________________________

____

Utilities (i.e., wi-fi, electricity, etc.;)

Website:____

Username:______________________________________

Password:______________________________________

Last 3 Passwords:__________________________________

Important to Note (i.e. date reminder):____________________

Website:____

Username:______________________________________

Password:______________________________________

Last 3 Passwords:__________________________________

Important to Note (i.e. date reminder):____________________

Website:____

Username:______________________________________

Password:______________________________________

Last 3 Passwords:__________________________________

Important to Note (i.e. date reminder):____________________

Utilities (i.e., wi-fi, electricity, etc.;)

Website:____

Username:______________________________________

Password:_______________________________________

Last 3 Passwords:_________________________________

Important to Note (i.e. date reminder):____________________

____

Website:____

Username:______________________________________

Password:_______________________________________

Last 3 Passwords:_________________________________

Important to Note (i.e. date reminder):____________________

____

Website:____

Username:______________________________________

Password:_______________________________________

Last 3 Passwords:_________________________________

Important to Note (i.e. date reminder):____________________

____

Utilities (i.e., wi-fi, electricity, etc.;)

Website:____

Username:____

Password:____

Last 3 Passwords:____

Important to Note (i.e. date reminder):_________________________

____

Website:____

Username:____

Password:____

Last 3 Passwords:____

Important to Note (i.e. date reminder):_________________________

____

Website:____

Username:____

Password:____

Last 3 Passwords:____

Important to Note (i.e. date reminder):_________________________

____

Utilities (i.e., wi-fi, electricity, etc.;)

Website:____

Username:______________________________________

Password:______________________________________

Last 3 Passwords:__________________________________

Important to Note (i.e. date reminder):____________________

____

Website:____

Username:______________________________________

Password:______________________________________

Last 3 Passwords:__________________________________

Important to Note (i.e. date reminder):____________________

____

Website:____

Username:______________________________________

Password:______________________________________

Last 3 Passwords:__________________________________

Important to Note (i.e. date reminder):____________________

____

Utilities (i.e., wi-fi, electricity, etc.;)

Website:____

Username:______________________________________

Password:_______________________________________

Last 3 Passwords:__________________________________

Important to Note (i.e. date reminder):____________________

____

Website:____

Username:______________________________________

Password:_______________________________________

Last 3 Passwords:__________________________________

Important to Note (i.e. date reminder):____________________

____

Website:____

Username:______________________________________

Password:_______________________________________

Last 3 Passwords:__________________________________

Important to Note (i.e. date reminder):____________________

____

Education (i.e., school log-in portals, school reminder applications)

Website:____

Username:______________________________________

Password:______________________________________

Last 3 Passwords:________________________________

Important to Note (i.e. date reminder):____________________

____

Website:____

Username:______________________________________

Password:______________________________________

Last 3 Passwords:________________________________

Important to Note (i.e. date reminder):____________________

____

Website:____

Username:______________________________________

Password:______________________________________

Last 3 Passwords:________________________________

Important to Note (i.e. date reminder):____________________

____

Education (i.e., school log-in portals, school reminder applications)

Website:____

Username:______________________________________

Password:______________________________________

Last 3 Passwords:__________________________________

Important to Note (i.e. date reminder):______________________

____

Website:____

Username:______________________________________

Password:______________________________________

Last 3 Passwords:__________________________________

Important to Note (i.e. date reminder):______________________

____

Website:____

Username:______________________________________

Password:______________________________________

Last 3 Passwords:__________________________________

Important to Note (i.e. date reminder):______________________

____

Education (i.e., school log-in portals, school reminder applications)

Website:____

Username:______________________________________

Password:_______________________________________

Last 3 Passwords:__________________________________

Important to Note (i.e. date reminder):____________________

____

Website:____

Username:______________________________________

Password:_______________________________________

Last 3 Passwords:__________________________________

Important to Note (i.e. date reminder):____________________

____

Website:____

Username:______________________________________

Password:_______________________________________

Last 3 Passwords:__________________________________

Important to Note (i.e. date reminder):____________________

____

Education (i.e., school log-in portals, school reminder applications)

Website:____

Username:______________________________________

Password:_______________________________________

Last 3 Passwords:__________________________________

Important to Note (i.e. date reminder):____________________

____

Website:____

Username:______________________________________

Password:_______________________________________

Last 3 Passwords:__________________________________

Important to Note (i.e. date reminder):____________________

____

Website:____

Username:______________________________________

Password:_______________________________________

Last 3 Passwords:__________________________________

Important to Note (i.e. date reminder):____________________

____

Education (i.e., school log-in portals, school reminder applications)

Website:____

Username:______________________________________

Password:_______________________________________

Last 3 Passwords:_________________________________

Important to Note (i.e. date reminder):____________________

____

Website:____

Username:______________________________________

Password:_______________________________________

Last 3 Passwords:_________________________________

Important to Note (i.e. date reminder):____________________

____

Website:____

Username:______________________________________

Password:_______________________________________

Last 3 Passwords:_________________________________

Important to Note (i.e. date reminder):____________________

____

Education (i.e., school log-in portals, school reminder applications)

Website:____

Username:______________________________________

Password:_______________________________________

Last 3 Passwords:_________________________________

Important to Note (i.e. date reminder):____________________

____

Website:____

Username:______________________________________

Password:_______________________________________

Last 3 Passwords:_________________________________

Important to Note (i.e. date reminder):____________________

____

Website:____

Username:______________________________________

Password:_______________________________________

Last 3 Passwords:_________________________________

Important to Note (i.e. date reminder):____________________

____

Education (i.e., school log-in portals, school reminder applications)

Website:____

Username:____

Password:____

Last 3 Passwords:_______________________________________

Important to Note (i.e. date reminder):_______________________

____

Website:____

Username:____

Password:____

Last 3 Passwords:_______________________________________

Important to Note (i.e. date reminder):_______________________

____

Website:____

Username:____

Password:____

Last 3 Passwords:_______________________________________

Important to Note (i.e. date reminder):_______________________

____

Education (i.e., school log-in portals, school reminder applications)

Website:____

Username:______________________________________

Password:_______________________________________

Last 3 Passwords:_________________________________

Important to Note (i.e. date reminder):____________________

____

Website:____

Username:______________________________________

Password:_______________________________________

Last 3 Passwords:_________________________________

Important to Note (i.e. date reminder):____________________

____

Website:____

Username:______________________________________

Password:_______________________________________

Last 3 Passwords:_________________________________

Important to Note (i.e. date reminder):____________________

____

Education (i.e., school log-in portals, school reminder applications)

Website:____

Username:_______________________________________

Password:_______________________________________

Last 3 Passwords:__________________________________

Important to Note (i.e. date reminder):_____________________

____

Website:____

Username:_______________________________________

Password:_______________________________________

Last 3 Passwords:__________________________________

Important to Note (i.e. date reminder):_____________________

____

Website:____

Username:_______________________________________

Password:_______________________________________

Last 3 Passwords:__________________________________

Important to Note (i.e. date reminder):_____________________

____

Education (i.e., school log-in portals, school reminder applications)

Website:____

Username:______________________________________

Password:______________________________________

Last 3 Passwords:__________________________________

Important to Note (i.e. date reminder):____________________

____

Website:____

Username:______________________________________

Password:______________________________________

Last 3 Passwords:__________________________________

Important to Note (i.e. date reminder):____________________

____

Website:____

Username:______________________________________

Password:______________________________________

Last 3 Passwords:__________________________________

Important to Note (i.e. date reminder):____________________

____

Entertainment (i.e., streaming services, etc.;)

Website:______________________________________

Username:_____________________________________

Password:______________________________________

Last 3 Passwords:________________________________

Important to Note (i.e. date reminder):____________________

____

Website:______________________________________

Username:_____________________________________

Password:______________________________________

Last 3 Passwords:________________________________

Important to Note (i.e. date reminder):____________________

____

Website:______________________________________

Username:_____________________________________

Password:______________________________________

Last 3 Passwords:________________________________

Important to Note (i.e. date reminder):____________________

____

Entertainment (i.e., streaming services, etc.;)

Website:____

Username:______________________________________

Password:______________________________________

Last 3 Passwords:__________________________________

Important to Note (i.e. date reminder):____________________

____

Website:____

Username:______________________________________

Password:______________________________________

Last 3 Passwords:__________________________________

Important to Note (i.e. date reminder):____________________

____

Website:____

Username:______________________________________

Password:______________________________________

Last 3 Passwords:__________________________________

Important to Note (i.e. date reminder):____________________

____

Entertainment (i.e., streaming services, etc.;)

Website:______________________________________

Username:_____________________________________

Password:_____________________________________

Last 3 Passwords:_______________________________

Important to Note (i.e. date reminder):__________________

Website:______________________________________

Username:_____________________________________

Password:_____________________________________

Last 3 Passwords:_______________________________

Important to Note (i.e. date reminder):__________________

Website:______________________________________

Username:_____________________________________

Password:_____________________________________

Last 3 Passwords:_______________________________

Important to Note (i.e. date reminder):__________________

Entertainment (i.e., streaming services, etc.;)

Website:____

Username:_______________________________________

Password:_______________________________________

Last 3 Passwords:__________________________________

Important to Note (i.e. date reminder):____________________

____

Website:____

Username:_______________________________________

Password:_______________________________________

Last 3 Passwords:__________________________________

Important to Note (i.e. date reminder):____________________

____

Website:____

Username:_______________________________________

Password:_______________________________________

Last 3 Passwords:__________________________________

Important to Note (i.e. date reminder):____________________

____

Entertainment (i.e., streaming services, etc.;)

Website:____________________________________

Username:___________________________________

Password:____________________________________

Last 3 Passwords:_______________________________

Important to Note (i.e. date reminder):___________________

____

Website:____________________________________

Username:___________________________________

Password:____________________________________

Last 3 Passwords:_______________________________

Important to Note (i.e. date reminder):___________________

____

Website:____________________________________

Username:___________________________________

Password:____________________________________

Last 3 Passwords:_______________________________

Important to Note (i.e. date reminder):___________________

____

Entertainment (i.e., streaming services, etc.;)

Website:____

Username:______________________________________

Password:_______________________________________

Last 3 Passwords:________________________________

Important to Note (i.e. date reminder):____________________

____

Website:____

Username:______________________________________

Password:_______________________________________

Last 3 Passwords:________________________________

Important to Note (i.e. date reminder):____________________

____

Website:____

Username:______________________________________

Password:_______________________________________

Last 3 Passwords:________________________________

Important to Note (i.e. date reminder):____________________

____

Entertainment (i.e., streaming services, etc.;)

Website:____

Username:______________________________________

Password:______________________________________

Last 3 Passwords:__________________________________

Important to Note (i.e. date reminder):____________________

Website:____

Username:______________________________________

Password:______________________________________

Last 3 Passwords:__________________________________

Important to Note (i.e. date reminder):____________________

Website:____

Username:______________________________________

Password:______________________________________

Last 3 Passwords:__________________________________

Important to Note (i.e. date reminder):____________________

Entertainment (i.e., streaming services, etc.;)

Website:____

Username:____

Password:____

Last 3 Passwords:______________________________________

Important to Note (i.e. date reminder):_______________________

____

Website:____

Username:____

Password:____

Last 3 Passwords:______________________________________

Important to Note (i.e. date reminder):_______________________

____

Website:____

Username:____

Password:____

Last 3 Passwords:______________________________________

Important to Note (i.e. date reminder):_______________________

____

Entertainment (i.e., streaming services, etc.;)

Website:____

Username:______________________________________

Password:_______________________________________

Last 3 Passwords:__________________________________

Important to Note (i.e. date reminder):____________________

____

Website:____

Username:______________________________________

Password:_______________________________________

Last 3 Passwords:__________________________________

Important to Note (i.e. date reminder):____________________

____

Website:____

Username:______________________________________

Password:_______________________________________

Last 3 Passwords:__________________________________

Important to Note (i.e. date reminder):____________________

____

Entertainment (i.e., streaming services, etc.;)

Website:____

Username:____

Password:____

Last 3 Passwords:____________________________________

Important to Note (i.e. date reminder):______________________

____

Website:____

Username:____

Password:____

Last 3 Passwords:____________________________________

Important to Note (i.e. date reminder):______________________

____

Website:____

Username:____

Password:____

Last 3 Passwords:____________________________________

Important to Note (i.e. date reminder):______________________

____

Shopping & Food (i.e., grocery delivery, food delivery services, online shopping)

Website:________________________________

Username:________________________________

Password:________________________________

Last 3 Passwords:____________________________

Important to Note (i.e. date reminder):________________

____

Website:________________________________

Username:________________________________

Password:________________________________

Last 3 Passwords:____________________________

Important to Note (i.e. date reminder):________________

____

Website:________________________________

Username:________________________________

Password:________________________________

Last 3 Passwords:____________________________

Important to Note (i.e. date reminder):________________

____

Shopping & Food (i.e., grocery delivery, food delivery services, online shopping)

Website:____

Username:______________________________________

Password:______________________________________

Last 3 Passwords:__________________________________

Important to Note (i.e. date reminder):______________________

____

Website:____

Username:______________________________________

Password:______________________________________

Last 3 Passwords:__________________________________

Important to Note (i.e. date reminder):______________________

____

Website:____

Username:______________________________________

Password:______________________________________

Last 3 Passwords:__________________________________

Important to Note (i.e. date reminder):______________________

____

Shopping & Food (i.e., grocery delivery, food delivery services, online shopping)

Website:____

Username:____

Password:____

Last 3 Passwords:__________________________________

Important to Note (i.e. date reminder):____________________

____

Website:____

Username:____

Password:____

Last 3 Passwords:__________________________________

Important to Note (i.e. date reminder):____________________

____

Website:____

Username:____

Password:____

Last 3 Passwords:__________________________________

Important to Note (i.e. date reminder):____________________

____

Shopping & Food (i.e., grocery delivery, food delivery services, online shopping)

Website:____

Username:______________________________________

Password:_______________________________________

Last 3 Passwords:_________________________________

Important to Note (i.e. date reminder):____________________

____

Website:____

Username:______________________________________

Password:_______________________________________

Last 3 Passwords:_________________________________

Important to Note (i.e. date reminder):____________________

____

Website:____

Username:______________________________________

Password:_______________________________________

Last 3 Passwords:_________________________________

Important to Note (i.e. date reminder):____________________

____

Shopping & Food (i.e., grocery delivery, food delivery services, online shopping)

Website:____

Username:____

Password:____

Last 3 Passwords:______________________________________

Important to Note (i.e. date reminder):____________________

____

Website:____

Username:____

Password:____

Last 3 Passwords:______________________________________

Important to Note (i.e. date reminder):____________________

____

Website:____

Username:____

Password:____

Last 3 Passwords:______________________________________

Important to Note (i.e. date reminder):____________________

____

Shopping & Food (i.e., grocery delivery, food delivery services, online shopping)

Website:____

Username:______________________________________

Password:______________________________________

Last 3 Passwords:_________________________________

Important to Note (i.e. date reminder):____________________

____

Website:____

Username:______________________________________

Password:______________________________________

Last 3 Passwords:_________________________________

Important to Note (i.e. date reminder):____________________

____

Website:____

Username:______________________________________

Password:______________________________________

Last 3 Passwords:_________________________________

Important to Note (i.e. date reminder):____________________

____

Shopping & Food (i.e., grocery delivery, food delivery services, online shopping)

Website:____

Username:______________________________________

Password:______________________________________

Last 3 Passwords:__________________________________

Important to Note (i.e. date reminder):____________________

Website:____

Username:______________________________________

Password:______________________________________

Last 3 Passwords:__________________________________

Important to Note (i.e. date reminder):____________________

Website:____

Username:______________________________________

Password:______________________________________

Last 3 Passwords:__________________________________

Important to Note (i.e. date reminder):____________________

Shopping & Food (i.e., grocery delivery, food delivery services, online shopping)

Website:____

Username:______________________________________

Password:______________________________________

Last 3 Passwords:_________________________________

Important to Note (i.e. date reminder):____________________

____

Website:____

Username:______________________________________

Password:______________________________________

Last 3 Passwords:_________________________________

Important to Note (i.e. date reminder):____________________

____

Website:____

Username:______________________________________

Password:______________________________________

Last 3 Passwords:_________________________________

Important to Note (i.e. date reminder):____________________

____

Shopping & Food (i.e., grocery delivery, food delivery services, online shopping)

Website:____

Username:______________________________________

Password:______________________________________

Last 3 Passwords:_________________________________

Important to Note (i.e. date reminder):____________________

____

Website:____

Username:______________________________________

Password:______________________________________

Last 3 Passwords:_________________________________

Important to Note (i.e. date reminder):____________________

____

Website:____

Username:______________________________________

Password:______________________________________

Last 3 Passwords:_________________________________

Important to Note (i.e. date reminder):____________________

____

Shopping & Food (i.e., grocery delivery, food delivery services, online shopping)

Website:____

Username:______________________________________

Password:_______________________________________

Last 3 Passwords:__________________________________

Important to Note (i.e. date reminder):_______________________

____

Website:____

Username:______________________________________

Password:_______________________________________

Last 3 Passwords:__________________________________

Important to Note (i.e. date reminder):_______________________

____

Website:____

Username:______________________________________

Password:_______________________________________

Last 3 Passwords:__________________________________

Important to Note (i.e. date reminder):_______________________

____

Travel (i.e., travel sites, airlines, etc.;)

Website:____

Username:_______________________________________

Password:_______________________________________

Last 3 Passwords:__________________________________

Important to Note (i.e. date reminder):______________________

____

Website:____

Username:_______________________________________

Password:_______________________________________

Last 3 Passwords:__________________________________

Important to Note (i.e. date reminder):______________________

____

Website:____

Username:_______________________________________

Password:_______________________________________

Last 3 Passwords:__________________________________

Important to Note (i.e. date reminder):______________________

____

Travel (i.e., travel sites, airlines, etc.;)

Website:____

Username:______________________________________

Password:_______________________________________

Last 3 Passwords:__________________________________

Important to Note (i.e. date reminder):____________________

____

Website:____

Username:______________________________________

Password:_______________________________________

Last 3 Passwords:__________________________________

Important to Note (i.e. date reminder):____________________

____

Website:____

Username:______________________________________

Password:_______________________________________

Last 3 Passwords:__________________________________

Important to Note (i.e. date reminder):____________________

____

Travel (i.e., travel sites, airlines, etc.;)

Website:____

Username:______________________________________

Password:______________________________________

Last 3 Passwords:_________________________________

Important to Note (i.e. date reminder):____________________

____

Website:____

Username:______________________________________

Password:______________________________________

Last 3 Passwords:_________________________________

Important to Note (i.e. date reminder):____________________

____

Website:____

Username:______________________________________

Password:______________________________________

Last 3 Passwords:_________________________________

Important to Note (i.e. date reminder):____________________

____

Travel (i.e., travel sites, airlines, etc.;)

Website:______________________________________

Username:____________________________________

Password:_____________________________________

Last 3 Passwords:________________________________

Important to Note (i.e. date reminder):____________________

Website:______________________________________

Username:____________________________________

Password:_____________________________________

Last 3 Passwords:________________________________

Important to Note (i.e. date reminder):____________________

Website:______________________________________

Username:____________________________________

Password:_____________________________________

Last 3 Passwords:________________________________

Important to Note (i.e. date reminder):____________________

Travel (i.e., travel sites, airlines, etc.;)

Website:____

Username:______________________________________

Password:_______________________________________

Last 3 Passwords:_________________________________

Important to Note (i.e. date reminder):____________________

____

Website:____

Username:______________________________________

Password:_______________________________________

Last 3 Passwords:_________________________________

Important to Note (i.e. date reminder):____________________

____

Website:____

Username:______________________________________

Password:_______________________________________

Last 3 Passwords:_________________________________

Important to Note (i.e. date reminder):____________________

____

Travel (i.e., travel sites, airlines, etc.;)

Website:____

Username:______________________________________

Password:______________________________________

Last 3 Passwords:________________________________

Important to Note (i.e. date reminder):____________________

____

Website:____

Username:______________________________________

Password:______________________________________

Last 3 Passwords:________________________________

Important to Note (i.e. date reminder):____________________

____

Website:____

Username:______________________________________

Password:______________________________________

Last 3 Passwords:________________________________

Important to Note (i.e. date reminder):____________________

____

Travel (i.e., travel sites, airlines, etc.;)

Website:____

Username:______________________________________

Password:_______________________________________

Last 3 Passwords:__________________________________

Important to Note (i.e. date reminder):______________________

____

Website:____

Username:______________________________________

Password:_______________________________________

Last 3 Passwords:__________________________________

Important to Note (i.e. date reminder):______________________

____

Website:____

Username:______________________________________

Password:_______________________________________

Last 3 Passwords:__________________________________

Important to Note (i.e. date reminder):______________________

____

Travel (i.e., travel sites, airlines, etc.;)

Website:____

Username:______________________________________

Password:_______________________________________

Last 3 Passwords:__________________________________

Important to Note (i.e. date reminder):____________________

____

Website:____

Username:______________________________________

Password:_______________________________________

Last 3 Passwords:__________________________________

Important to Note (i.e. date reminder):____________________

____

Website:____

Username:______________________________________

Password:_______________________________________

Last 3 Passwords:__________________________________

Important to Note (i.e. date reminder):____________________

____

Travel (i.e., travel sites, airlines, etc.;)

Website:____

Username:______________________________________

Password:_______________________________________

Last 3 Passwords:_________________________________

Important to Note (i.e. date reminder):____________________

____

Website:____

Username:______________________________________

Password:_______________________________________

Last 3 Passwords:_________________________________

Important to Note (i.e. date reminder):____________________

____

Website:____

Username:______________________________________

Password:_______________________________________

Last 3 Passwords:_________________________________

Important to Note (i.e. date reminder):____________________

____

Travel (i.e., travel sites, airlines, etc.;)

Website:____

Username:______________________________________

Password:_______________________________________

Last 3 Passwords:_________________________________

Important to Note (i.e. date reminder):____________________

____

Website:____

Username:______________________________________

Password:_______________________________________

Last 3 Passwords:_________________________________

Important to Note (i.e. date reminder):____________________

____

Website:____

Username:______________________________________

Password:_______________________________________

Last 3 Passwords:_________________________________

Important to Note (i.e. date reminder):____________________

____

Health & Fitness (i.e. medical information, patient records, fitness subscriptions, etc)

Website:____

Username:______________________________________

Password:______________________________________

Last 3 Passwords:________________________________

Important to Note (i.e. date reminder):____________________

____

Website:____

Username:______________________________________

Password:______________________________________

Last 3 Passwords:________________________________

Important to Note (i.e. date reminder):____________________

____

Website:____

Username:______________________________________

Password:______________________________________

Last 3 Passwords:________________________________

Important to Note (i.e. date reminder):____________________

____

Health & Fitness (i.e. medical information, patient records, fitness subscriptions, etc)

Website:____

Username:______________________________________

Password:______________________________________

Last 3 Passwords:__________________________________

Important to Note (i.e. date reminder):____________________

____

Website:____

Username:______________________________________

Password:______________________________________

Last 3 Passwords:__________________________________

Important to Note (i.e. date reminder):____________________

____

Website:____

Username:______________________________________

Password:______________________________________

Last 3 Passwords:__________________________________

Important to Note (i.e. date reminder):____________________

____

Health & Fitness (i.e. medical information, patient records, fitness subscriptions, etc)

Website:____

Username:____

Password:____

Last 3 Passwords:____________________________________

Important to Note (i.e. date reminder):____________________

____

Website:____

Username:____

Password:____

Last 3 Passwords:____________________________________

Important to Note (i.e. date reminder):____________________

____

Website:____

Username:____

Password:____

Last 3 Passwords:____________________________________

Important to Note (i.e. date reminder):____________________

____

Health & Fitness (i.e. medical information, patient records, fitness subscriptions, etc)

Website:____

Username:______________________________________

Password:______________________________________

Last 3 Passwords:__________________________________

Important to Note (i.e. date reminder):_____________________

____

Website:____

Username:______________________________________

Password:______________________________________

Last 3 Passwords:__________________________________

Important to Note (i.e. date reminder):_____________________

____

Website:____

Username:______________________________________

Password:______________________________________

Last 3 Passwords:__________________________________

Important to Note (i.e. date reminder):_____________________

____

Health & Fitness (i.e. medical information, patient records, fitness subscriptions, etc)

Website:____

Username:_______________________________________

Password:_______________________________________

Last 3 Passwords:_________________________________

Important to Note (i.e. date reminder):____________________

Website:____

Username:_______________________________________

Password:_______________________________________

Last 3 Passwords:_________________________________

Important to Note (i.e. date reminder):____________________

Website:____

Username:_______________________________________

Password:_______________________________________

Last 3 Passwords:_________________________________

Important to Note (i.e. date reminder):____________________

Health & Fitness (i.e. medical information, patient records, fitness subscriptions, etc)

Website:____

Username:______________________________________

Password:______________________________________

Last 3 Passwords:________________________________

Important to Note (i.e. date reminder):____________________

____

Website:____

Username:______________________________________

Password:______________________________________

Last 3 Passwords:________________________________

Important to Note (i.e. date reminder):____________________

____

Website:____

Username:______________________________________

Password:______________________________________

Last 3 Passwords:________________________________

Important to Note (i.e. date reminder):____________________

____

Health & Fitness (i.e. medical information, patient records, fitness subscriptions, etc)

Website:____

Username:______________________________________

Password:______________________________________

Last 3 Passwords:________________________________

Important to Note (i.e. date reminder):____________________

____

Website:____

Username:______________________________________

Password:______________________________________

Last 3 Passwords:________________________________

Important to Note (i.e. date reminder):____________________

____

Website:____

Username:______________________________________

Password:______________________________________

Last 3 Passwords:________________________________

Important to Note (i.e. date reminder):____________________

____

Health & Fitness (i.e. medical information, patient records, fitness subscriptions, etc)

Website:____

Username:______________________________________

Password:_______________________________________

Last 3 Passwords:__________________________________

Important to Note (i.e. date reminder):____________________

____

Website:____

Username:______________________________________

Password:_______________________________________

Last 3 Passwords:__________________________________

Important to Note (i.e. date reminder):____________________

____

Website:____

Username:______________________________________

Password:_______________________________________

Last 3 Passwords:__________________________________

Important to Note (i.e. date reminder):____________________

____

Health & Fitness (i.e. medical information, patient records, fitness subscriptions, etc)

Website:____

Username:____

Password:____

Last 3 Passwords:_______________________________________

Important to Note (i.e. date reminder):____________________

____

Website:____

Username:____

Password:____

Last 3 Passwords:_______________________________________

Important to Note (i.e. date reminder):____________________

____

Website:____

Username:____

Password:____

Last 3 Passwords:_______________________________________

Important to Note (i.e. date reminder):____________________

____

Health & Fitness (i.e. medical information, patient records, fitness subscriptions, etc)

Website:____

Username:_______________________________________

Password:_______________________________________

Last 3 Passwords:__________________________________

Important to Note (i.e. date reminder):____________________

____

Website:____

Username:_______________________________________

Password:_______________________________________

Last 3 Passwords:__________________________________

Important to Note (i.e. date reminder):____________________

____

Website:____

Username:_______________________________________

Password:_______________________________________

Last 3 Passwords:__________________________________

Important to Note (i.e. date reminder):____________________

____

Other (i.e., Apps)

Website:____

Username:______________________________________

Password:______________________________________

Last 3 Passwords:__________________________________

Important to Note (i.e. date reminder):____________________

____

Website:____

Username:______________________________________

Password:______________________________________

Last 3 Passwords:__________________________________

Important to Note (i.e. date reminder):____________________

____

Website:____

Username:______________________________________

Password:______________________________________

Last 3 Passwords:__________________________________

Important to Note (i.e. date reminder):____________________

____

Other (i.e., Apps)

Website:____

Username:______________________________________

Password:_______________________________________

Last 3 Passwords:_________________________________

Important to Note (i.e. date reminder):____________________

____

Website:____

Username:______________________________________

Password:_______________________________________

Last 3 Passwords:_________________________________

Important to Note (i.e. date reminder):____________________

____

Website:____

Username:______________________________________

Password:_______________________________________

Last 3 Passwords:_________________________________

Important to Note (i.e. date reminder):____________________

____

Other (i.e., Apps)

Website:____

Username:______________________________________

Password:______________________________________

Last 3 Passwords:________________________________

Important to Note (i.e. date reminder):____________________

Website:____

Username:______________________________________

Password:______________________________________

Last 3 Passwords:________________________________

Important to Note (i.e. date reminder):____________________

Website:____

Username:______________________________________

Password:______________________________________

Last 3 Passwords:________________________________

Important to Note (i.e. date reminder):____________________

Other (i.e., Apps)

Website:____

Username:______________________________________

Password:______________________________________

Last 3 Passwords:_________________________________

Important to Note (i.e. date reminder):____________________

____

Website:____

Username:______________________________________

Password:______________________________________

Last 3 Passwords:_________________________________

Important to Note (i.e. date reminder):____________________

____

Website:____

Username:______________________________________

Password:______________________________________

Last 3 Passwords:_________________________________

Important to Note (i.e. date reminder):____________________

____

Other (i.e., Apps)

Website:________________________________

Username:_______________________________

Password:_______________________________

Last 3 Passwords:__________________________

Important to Note (i.e. date reminder):________________

____

Website:________________________________

Username:_______________________________

Password:_______________________________

Last 3 Passwords:__________________________

Important to Note (i.e. date reminder):________________

____

Website:________________________________

Username:_______________________________

Password:_______________________________

Last 3 Passwords:__________________________

Important to Note (i.e. date reminder):________________

____

Other (i.e., Apps)

Website:____

Username:______________________________________

Password:_______________________________________

Last 3 Passwords:________________________________

Important to Note (i.e. date reminder):____________________

____

Website:____

Username:______________________________________

Password:_______________________________________

Last 3 Passwords:________________________________

Important to Note (i.e. date reminder):____________________

____

Website:____

Username:______________________________________

Password:_______________________________________

Last 3 Passwords:________________________________

Important to Note (i.e. date reminder):____________________

____

Other (i.e., Apps)

Website:____

Username:______________________________________

Password:______________________________________

Last 3 Passwords:________________________________

Important to Note (i.e. date reminder):____________________

____

Website:____

Username:______________________________________

Password:______________________________________

Last 3 Passwords:________________________________

Important to Note (i.e. date reminder):____________________

____

Website:____

Username:______________________________________

Password:______________________________________

Last 3 Passwords:________________________________

Important to Note (i.e. date reminder):____________________

____

Other (i.e., Apps)

Website:____________________________________

Username:___________________________________

Password:___________________________________

Last 3 Passwords:______________________________

Important to Note (i.e. date reminder):___________________

____

Website:____________________________________

Username:___________________________________

Password:___________________________________

Last 3 Passwords:______________________________

Important to Note (i.e. date reminder):___________________

____

Website:____________________________________

Username:___________________________________

Password:___________________________________

Last 3 Passwords:______________________________

Important to Note (i.e. date reminder):___________________

____

Other (i.e., Apps)

Website:____

Username:______________________________________

Password:_______________________________________

Last 3 Passwords:________________________________

Important to Note (i.e. date reminder):____________________

Website:____

Username:______________________________________

Password:_______________________________________

Last 3 Passwords:________________________________

Important to Note (i.e. date reminder):____________________

Website:____

Username:______________________________________

Password:_______________________________________

Last 3 Passwords:________________________________

Important to Note (i.e. date reminder):____________________

Other (i.e., Apps)

Website:____

Username:______________________________________

Password:_______________________________________

Last 3 Passwords:__________________________________

Important to Note (i.e. date reminder):____________________

____

Website:____

Username:______________________________________

Password:_______________________________________

Last 3 Passwords:__________________________________

Important to Note (i.e. date reminder):____________________

____

Website:____

Username:______________________________________

Password:_______________________________________

Last 3 Passwords:__________________________________

Important to Note (i.e. date reminder):____________________

____

Passwords &Usernames that have been compromised

Website:____

Username:____

Password:____

Last 3 Passwords:____________________________________

Important to Note (i.e. date reminder):_____________________

____

Website:____

Username:____

Password:____

Last 3 Passwords:____________________________________

Important to Note (i.e. date reminder):_____________________

____

Website:____

Username:____

Password:____

Last 3 Passwords:____________________________________

Important to Note (i.e. date reminder):_____________________

____

Passwords &Usernames that have been compromised

Website:____________________________________

Username:___________________________________

Password:___________________________________

Last 3 Passwords:______________________________

Important to Note (i.e. date reminder):____________________

____

Website:____________________________________

Username:___________________________________

Password:___________________________________

Last 3 Passwords:______________________________

Important to Note (i.e. date reminder):____________________

____

Website:____________________________________

Username:___________________________________

Password:___________________________________

Last 3 Passwords:______________________________

Important to Note (i.e. date reminder):____________________

____

Passwords &Usernames that have been compromised

Website:____

Username:____

Password:____

Last 3 Passwords:___________________________________

Important to Note (i.e. date reminder):_________________

____

Website:____

Username:____

Password:____

Last 3 Passwords:___________________________________

Important to Note (i.e. date reminder):_________________

____

Website:____

Username:____

Password:____

Last 3 Passwords:___________________________________

Important to Note (i.e. date reminder):_________________

____

Passwords &Usernames that have been compromised

Website:____

Username:______________________________________

Password:_______________________________________

Last 3 Passwords:__________________________________

Important to Note (i.e. date reminder):____________________

____

Website:____

Username:______________________________________

Password:_______________________________________

Last 3 Passwords:__________________________________

Important to Note (i.e. date reminder):____________________

____

Website:____

Username:______________________________________

Password:_______________________________________

Last 3 Passwords:__________________________________

Important to Note (i.e. date reminder):____________________

____

Passwords &Usernames that have been compromised

Website:______________________________________

Username:_____________________________________

Password:______________________________________

Last 3 Passwords:_________________________________

Important to Note (i.e. date reminder):____________________

____

Website:______________________________________

Username:_____________________________________

Password:______________________________________

Last 3 Passwords:_________________________________

Important to Note (i.e. date reminder):____________________

____

Website:______________________________________

Username:_____________________________________

Password:______________________________________

Last 3 Passwords:_________________________________

Important to Note (i.e. date reminder):____________________

____

Passwords &Usernames that have been compromised

Website:____

Username:______________________________________

Password:_______________________________________

Last 3 Passwords:________________________________

Important to Note (i.e. date reminder):____________________

____

Website:____

Username:______________________________________

Password:_______________________________________

Last 3 Passwords:________________________________

Important to Note (i.e. date reminder):____________________

____

Website:____

Username:______________________________________

Password:_______________________________________

Last 3 Passwords:________________________________

Important to Note (i.e. date reminder):____________________

____

Made in the USA
Monee, IL
04 November 2026

67386070R10066